Copyright © 2024
Written by J.P. Connolly
All rights reserved

*For my family.
Thank you for believing.*

CONTENTS:

The Great Annual Reindeer Race

Oliver's Snowman

The Christmas Adventure

The Great Annual Reindeer Race

The Great Annual Reindeer Race

As the sun peeked out over the snowy wonderland of Santa's Village, the air hummed with excitement. In just one month's time, the highly anticipated Great Annual Reindeer Race would take place.

This race was a thrilling contest of skill and speed that determined which reindeer would help guide Santa's sleigh on Christmas Eve. For every reindeer, this was the ultimate honour and the experience of a lifetime.

In the lead-up to the event, each reindeer would train tirelessly, pushing themselves to the limit in the hope that they would be chosen that year. Chip was one of those reindeer.

Ever since he was tiny, all he ever dreamed of was being part of the team that led Santa's sleigh.

Now, I'm sure you've all figured out already that all reindeer love Christmas, but Chip—well, Chip REALLY loved it!

From the moment he could walk, he would peep through the window of Santa's workshop and watch with awe as the elves happily made toy after toy for all the boys and girls.

His eyes shone brightly as he watched the wrapping department carefully tie each sparkly bow, mesmerised by the piles of presents that gradually grew and grew in the corner of the workshop.

Presents of all shapes, colours, and sizes—magical gifts made with such love that he just knew they would bring happiness and joy to children all over the world on Christmas morning.

Every Christmas Eve, Chip would watch with amazement as the sleigh rose high into the crisp evening air, soaking up every magical moment. The bulging brown sack of presents tied with a golden rope, the happy jingling sound of the sleigh bells, Santa's jolly "HO HO HO" as he waved goodbye, and the pride and happiness shining from every reindeer chosen to help Santa on the most important night of the year.

Chip dreamed of flying. He imagined how it would feel to soar through the night sky, the wind whipping at his ears, his hooves miles from the ground. He imagined flying through a cloud, beside a friendly bird, or up close to the stars that twinkled so brightly in the sky. And to fly around the world on Christmas Eve, to be part of Santa's special team—he imagined there couldn't possibly be ANY better feeling.

So, just to set the record straight, reindeer can't fly. None of them can—not even Rudolph, Prancer, or Dancer. The only time reindeer can fly is on Christmas Eve, if they have been selected as part of the special Christmas sleigh team, and only after Santa has sprinkled them with his magical Christmas flying dust. Until then, the reindeer must practice running, jumping, and navigating with their hooves firmly on the ground.

With only one month to go, Chip got up extra early to ensure he had as much time as possible to train for the big event.

He started his day as usual with a run around the village, followed by a series of high jumps over his elf friend Ben, and then some heavy log-pulling to work on his strength. Chip wasn't the biggest of the reindeer or the strongest. Sometimes he was a little clumsy and managed to trip over his own hooves, but he was very determined and made sure he never, ever, missed a day of training.

After he had finished his usual morning workout, Chip decided to go and see how the other reindeer were getting on. First, he passed Bruce. Bruce was big, strong, and handsome, and Chip noticed that he was dragging twice as many logs as he had earlier that morning. Suddenly, Chip felt a pang of anxiety in his tummy.

Next, he passed Pippa. Pippa was running up and down the field behind the workshop at lightning speed, leaving little white puffs of snow behind her. "Wow," said Chip to himself. "I could never run as fast as Pippa!"

Then he passed Max, who was jumping back and forth over the tall red-and-white fence that surrounded the workshop. "That fence is double the size of Ben," he thought sadly to himself.

With a disappointed feeling creeping into his heart, Chip kicked his front right hoof in the snow, lowered his antlers, and began to head towards home.

"Hey, Chip, where are you going?" asked Ben. Ben was an elf and one of Chip's very best friends. "And why do you look so sad?" Ben tilted his head and looked worriedly at his friend.

"It's no good," said Chip sadly. "I'm never going to be as strong as Bruce, as fast as Pippa, or able to jump as high as Max. What's the point in training anymore? Santa won't pick me—why would he?"

Ben looked shocked at his friend's response. "But Chip, this is your dream; it's all you've ever wanted. Why would you give up now?" Chip shrugged. "I just don't think I'm special enough, I suppose," he confided honestly.

"Chip!" said Ben sincerely. "You are the kindest, most caring, and honest friend I could ever wish for. And you love Christmas far more than ANY reindeer I have ever met; Santa would be crazy not to pick you!"

Chip smiled shyly at his friend's kind words. "Thanks for trying to make me feel better," he said, "but I just don't think I'm fast or strong enough."

Ben patted the soft snow beside him. "Sit down and let me explain something to you," he said. "It's not only about being the fastest or the strongest. Santa needs his team to have a whole lot of different skills. They must be able to overcome any obstacle they come across on Christmas Eve, and trust me, they've come across a few over the years! They need wit, skill, endurance, and agility too."

Chip listened intently to his friend.

"Let me help you train, and I'm sure Santa

will pick you this year."

"Okay then," said Chip slowly, "if you really think I've got what it takes?"

"I most definitely do," said Ben, jumping up happily. "Now come on, we've got work to do!"

Over the next four weeks, Ben created a series of different, difficult challenges for his friend every single day. He was determined that if Chip could overcome these obstacles, he would be more than ready for The Great Annual Reindeer Race.

First, he started with The Icy Pond Dash. Chip's hooves clattered against the frozen surface, slipping as he worked hard to find his balance. Ben called out words of encouragement, urging his friend to find his rhythm. After many tries, Chip finally mastered the art of running across the ice, gliding almost gracefully with speed and skill.

Next came Forest Weaving. The trees were dense, their branches low and sharp. Chip had to run between them, moving his body with speed and agility. Ben watched, his heart pounding as Chip dashed past, dodging branches that seemed to reach out to scrape him. It wasn't easy; more than once, a stray branch tugged at Chip's antlers, but he never gave up. Each run made him faster and more nimble.

To build endurance, Ben designed the ultimate challenge: The Endurance Trek. He sent Chip on gruelling long-distance runs—scaling snowy hills, racing through valleys, and crossing ice-cold rivers. Chip's legs grew stronger with each step, and soon he could run for miles without tiring.

But it wasn't just about strength and speed. Chip had to be clever too. So Ben introduced The Obstacle Challenge. He scattered logs across Chip's path, set up tricky ice patches, and even dug hidden ditches. Chip had to stop, study the problem, and decide how to get through. Should he leap over, slide under, or find a way around? Each obstacle tested his wits, and slowly but surely, Chip began to master problem-solving on the go.

On one particularly windy day, Ben grinned as he introduced Wind Resistance Training. He laughed as he showed Chip how to lower his head and run full speed against the gusts that tried to push them back. Each time, Chip grew stronger, his legs powering through the wind. "You'll be ready for any weather, Chip!" Ben laughed as the wind howled around them.

As the final week of training approached, Ben had one last trick up his sleeve: The Midnight Run. In the darkness of the night, under a blanket of twinkling stars, Chip had to run through the forest. The trees loomed large, the paths barely visible, but Chip relied on his instincts, navigating the tricky terrain, even when the world around him was dark.

By the end of their training, Ben beamed with pride. Chip had become faster, stronger, and smarter than ever before. Every challenge, every icy dash, and every obstacle had helped make him a stronger competitor. As they stood together, staring out at the snowy landscape of Santa's Village, Ben knew his friend was ready.

The morning of the race had arrived. Chip woke up extra early with a fluttery feeling of butterflies in his tummy. He knew there was nothing else he could do now but try his best.

Chip had had such fun training with Ben over the last month and had learned how to do things he never thought possible. "When the race is over, win or lose, I'm going to make Ben a big thank-you cake," he thought happily to himself.

The reindeer began lining up at the starting line. Bruce was at the front, looking as strong and handsome as ever. Pippa was running in small circles, eager to begin, and Max was jumping up and down with an impatient look on his face. Chip took his place beside Rex, another small and friendly reindeer he knew from reindeer school. They smiled nervously at each other.

"Good morning, everyone!" Santa boomed happily from the sidelines. "The day has finally arrived. Welcome to our Great Annual Reindeer Race!" All the reindeer cheered enthusiastically while the elves clapped and shouted words of encouragement.

"As you well know, this race will determine which eight reindeer will guide my sleigh this year." Again, another huge cheer erupted. "I know you have all been training very hard, and I'm so proud of every one of you, but guiding my sleigh is no easy task. My chosen eight must be able to overcome any obstacles we come across on Christmas Eve. We must ensure that Christmas can prevail. You all have a tough race ahead of you, but if you can complete this course, then I know you can do it. I wish you all the best of luck!"

Santa clapped his hands and looked happily at his wonderful herd. There were fifty four reindeer competing this year, and they were all so excited and determined. He wished he could choose them all.

"On your marks!" shouted Santa. The

reindeer huddled together, pushing closer to the starting line. "Get set," continued Santa. Chip glanced over at Ben, who smiled and nodded confidently at his best friend.

"GOOOOOOOO!" Santa shouted.

Hooves thundered across the snow as the reindeer took off, their breath misting in the frosty air. Up ahead, the wind began to howl, pushing against the reindeer with all its might. Chip spotted Bruce struggling. Bruce was strong, but the gusts were too powerful for him.

"Bruce!" Chip called out, running alongside him. "Lower your head and use your strength to push through! Watch me."

Bruce nodded, his muscles straining as he lowered his head like Chip. Together, they leaned into the wind and powered through the gusts, the trees whipping past them.

"Wow, thank you Chip!" Bruce said genuinely "That was tough!"

As they approached the frozen pond, Chip saw Pippa ahead. She was skidding, sliding, and falling on the ice. Although she was a great runner, on the ice she simply couldn't manage to stay on her hooves. Chip raced over to her side.

"Pippa! Try stepping lighter! Keep your hooves flat on the ice like this!" Chip demonstrated, gliding over the frozen surface with ease, just like he'd practiced in The Icy Pond Dash.

Pippa watched and followed his lead, her hooves now steady on the ice. She grinned, picking up speed once again. "Thanks, Chip!" she called as they both crossed the pond safely.

Further down the track, a huge set of obstacles loomed ahead. Logs, ditches, and snow piles blocked the way. Chip saw Max pause in confusion, unsure of what to do.

"Max, over here!" Chip called. "That big log, jump over it, then slide under the next one! I'll show you!"

Max watched as Chip expertly jumped over the first log, then smoothly slid under the second. Max followed his lead, sailing over and under each obstacle with ease.

"That was perfect!" Chip cheered as they cleared the last hurdle.

"Thank you Chip!" Max shouted happily as he sped off.

But the race wasn't over yet. The path narrowed into the dense forest, where branches poked out like bony fingers, ready to jab at anyone who wasn't paying attention. Chip looked ahead and saw Rex, the smallest reindeer, struggling. The twigs were jabbing at his sides, and he winced with each step.

"Rex! Follow me!" Chip called.

He darted through the trees, weaving smoothly around the branches. Rex, still struggling, watched Chip's path and followed closely behind, copying his every move. Together, they dodged the poking branches, finally emerging from the thick forest.

"Thanks, Chip! I thought I'd be stuck in there forever!" Rex said gratefully.

The finish line was nearly in sight, and the crowd of elves was cheering louder than ever. Chip pushed onward. Normally, he would have been exhausted by now, but he found his endurance training was really helping. His legs felt strong and steady as he raced confidently through the snow. Suddenly, a deep, ice-cold river twinkled ahead of him. Lola, a young but very tall reindeer, was shivering in the centre, unable to move forward.

"Lola, are you okay?" called Chip.

"No," she cried. "I can't move, it's too cold."

"The longer you stay there, the colder you'll get," Chip replied as he swam over to her. "Now paddle with me, after three."

Chip swam beside her and encouraged her

to take her first paddle forward. She managed, then the second, then the third. Soon, they reached the edge of the icy water. Lola shook herself off as she quickly jumped out.

"Thank you so much, Chip!" she shivered. "Without you, I would have frozen!"

"No problem," Chip waved as he picked up speed once again.

He could now see the red and white finish line in the distance, and his heart sank a little as he noticed some other reindeer were ahead of him. He wasn't sure how many; he hoped not too many, but in his heart, he knew he had done the right thing by helping his friends. He put his antlers down and pushed on, determined to finish as quickly as he could.

"Yay!" cheered Ben as Chip burst through the finishing line. "You did it!"

Chip collapsed onto the soft white snow, breathing heavily. "Where did I come?" he asked nervously.

"You came in ninth place Chip," Ben said evenly. "But Chip, I'm so proud of you. You helped all those reindeer along the way. You should be so proud of yourself!"

"Ninth," Chip said sadly. "I won't get to guide the sleigh. But I suppose it did feel good to help my friends."

Ben put his arms around Chip's neck and gave him a huge hug. "I'm so proud of you, Chip," he said again warmly.

The two friends stood together at the finish line, waiting patiently for all the reindeer to complete the course. Next would be the awards ceremony. Each reindeer would be awarded a medal by Santa for taking part, and then he would announce his final eight. Santa appeared, his red coat gleaming against the snowy backdrop. The reindeer hushed as Santa approached, his warm smile lighting up his face.

"You all did wonderfully again this year,"

Santa boomed, his eyes twinkling with joy. "But as always, I must now announce the eight reindeer that will guide my sleigh this Christmas Eve."

The reindeer stood tall, their hearts racing with anticipation. Santa began calling out names.

"Bruce! Lucy! Milo! Milly! Max! Beau! Kera! And... Pippa!"

Chip's heart sank a little, but he smiled and clapped happily for his friends. He was still glad he'd helped Bruce, Max, and Pippa along the way, and was so excited for them to be able to guide the sleigh on Christmas Eve. And without him, Rex and Lola might sill not have even finished the race!

The crowd cheered and shouted their congratulations. "However, this year," Santa continued, his voice full of warmth, "I've decided to do something special."

A hushed silence fell over the crowd.
"This year, there will be nine reindeer guiding

my sleigh!"

The crowd gasped, and Chip's ears perked up in anticipation.

"Chip," Santa looked at him kindly. "You will lead the team this Christmas."

Chip blinked in disbelief. "Me?" he asked, his voice small.

Santa nodded, his eyes twinkling. "Yes, Chip. You showed great strength today, not just by running the race, but by stopping to help your friends along the way. Your kind heart and caring spirit are what make Christmas truly magical. And that's why you will lead my sleigh."

The other reindeer cheered, gathering around Chip and congratulating him. Bruce gave him a nudge, and Pippa beamed with pride. Max, Rex, Lola, and all the others joined in the celebration.

With his heart full of joy, Chip smiled up at Santa. This wasn't just a victory; it was a reminder that kindness and friendship are what truly matter. And now, Chip would fly at the very front of Santa's sleigh, guiding the way with his big, kind heart.

As Christmas Eve arrived, Chip proudly took his place at the front of the team of reindeer, his heart swelling with joy. He took a deep breath, soaking up the thrill of the moment, and looked back at Santa and his fellow reindeer, knowing that this was exactly where he was meant to be.

Suddenly, the world seemed to shift as he felt the air beneath his hooves and the sleigh begin to rise into the starry night sky. He glanced down and saw Ben waving excitedly, his face full of pride. In that moment, Chip had never felt so special, so important—his dream had finally come true.

As the sleigh soared higher, Chip's heart overflowed with gratitude for his friends, for the magic of the season, and for the chance to help make this the best Christmas ever.

The End.

Oliver's Snowman

Oliver's Snowman

"Wow!" exclaimed Oliver excitedly as he looked out of the window. During the night the snow had fallen thick and fast, and a beautiful soft layer of pure white snow was now beckoning him to step outside and play.

"Mum, Dad!" he called, "Can I go outside and play?"

"Yes, of course," replied his mother, "but not before you've had your breakfast, and be sure to wrap up warm, it's cold out there!"

Oliver raced into the kitchen and filled his bowl full to the top with his favourite Christmas cereal, spilling little snowflake puffs all over the kitchen countertop as he did so. With his eyes focused solely on the tantalising white carpet outside, he spooned his cereal into his mouth with lightning speed, until quick as a flash his bowl was empty.
Pulling on his boots, coat, gloves, scarf and

hat, he raced outside into the fresh, morning air. Oliver could feel his feet sinking deep into the snow below him, making a delicious, crunching sound that filled him with happiness.

Oliver loved December. He loved the snow. He loved cozy, dark evenings snuggled under a blanket watching Christmas movies with his family.

He loved the delicious smell of his Mum's special Christmas cookies that wafted out from the kitchen, and the mesmerising twinkle of their Christmas tree.

After about five minutes of running and jumping in the snow, inspecting how big and deep his footprints could be, Oliver decided that he would build a snowman.

First he rolled two big white snowballs, stacking them one on top of the other to create the snowman's body. Then he made another for his head. Looking around he caught sight of some broken branches laying on the ground. Oliver ran over, inspected them, and selected two similar sized ones to use for his snowman's arms. Next, he searched around and found a collection of smooth brown stones from his mother's flower bed. He was sure she wouldn't mind him borrowing them for a while.

Oliver placed the biggest stones in a straight line along the snowman's belly to look like buttons, then he added two more for his eyes, one for his nose and created a big upturned smile using the final smaller ones.

He unravelled his warm, green, knitted scarf and wrapped it carefully around the snowman's neck. Finally, with a triumphant smile, he pulled off his red woolly hat and placed it on top of the snowman's head.

Pleased with all his hard work Oliver stepped back to admire his creation. Oliver looked from the left, then he looked from the right, then he walked the whole way around the back of the snowman and back to his original starting place. He couldn't quite put his finger on it, but he he knew something was missing. He stared at the snowman's friendly face, with his big, upturned smile, but somehow the snowman just didn't look truly happy to him.

It was then that Oliver had an idea. He went racing back into the house, and sped upstairs to his bedroom. He opened the top drawer of his desk and began rummaging around. "Yes!" he said as he pulled out a big, shiny red button. It had fallen off of one of his favourite Christmas jumpers. It was so warm and cozy, every time he wore it, he instantly felt Christmassy and warm inside.

Next, he ran into the kitchen and grabbed a carrot from the fridge. "This will work better as a nose," he thought.

Running back outside, Oliver carefully removed the snowman's stone nose and replaced it with the carrot. Then, he gently placed the shiny red button onto the snowman's chest—he had given him a heart. Now, his snowman would be perfect. Stepping back to assess his work, Oliver was sure that both he and his snowman would now be happy with these final, finishing touches.

Suddenly, the wind picked up, and the snow began to fall in delicate, swirling flakes, dancing through the air like tiny crystals. Oliver shivered. Without his hat and scarf to keep him warm, he was starting to feel a little bit chilly. He pulled his jacket tightly around his waist and glanced back towards the kitchen door, considering going back inside for a while.

Then, out of nowhere, he heard something move behind him. Quick as a flash, Oliver spun around to see where the noise was coming from. To his complete surprise, his snowman was standing there scratching his head! Oliver rubbed his eyes and looked again, sure that it must just have been his imagination.

But it wasn't.... his snowman was moving, his snowman was smiling, his snowman was blinking, and most crazy of all his snowman was SPEAKING!

"Hello," said the snowman. "My name's Jake, Jake Frost. What's yours?"

"Errrrr… Oliver," Oliver stammered, not wanting to sound rude but not really knowing what the correct social etiquette was for when talking to a snowman.

"How, err, I mean why, err, I mean how… how are you talking to me?" Oliver stammered, barely able to put a sentence together.

"Well," replied Jake, "that was a bit of a mystery to me too! It's very rare for a snowman to be able to talk to his human. It did happen to my brother Jack once, or so he told us, but we never really knew if he was telling the truth or not!"

Oliver stared at the snowman, stunned, still quite unable to believe what was happening.

"So, how old are you?" Oliver asked. "Do snowmen have an age?"

"Yes, of course," Jake replied. "In our world, we go to school, we have friends, we play, just like you do."

Oliver's eyes widened as the snowman continued chatting quite happily. "So I'm nine. How old are you?"

"I'm nine too," Oliver said, still quite taken aback that he was actually having a conversation with a snowman he'd just built in his back garden.

"So, why do you think you came to life in MY garden?" Oliver asked, a puzzled look on his face. "I mean, of course I'm really happy you have, but… why?"

Jake looked down at his snow body and caught sight of the big shiny red button that Oliver had used to give him a heart.

"It could be because you gave me a heart," he said unsurely, "but I'm sure it can't just be because of that," he shrugged. "There is only a really special kind of magic that can bring a snowman from his world to yours, so we had better make the most of it before I have to go home again!"

"OK," Oliver smiled excitedly. "Well, let me show you around!"

He gently grabbed hold of Jake's wonky twig arm, and together they ran through the snow. Oliver showed Jake the big, deep footprints he could make in the snow, but without feet, Jake found this game a little bit difficult to master!

"Let's make snow angels then!" Oliver exclaimed as he threw himself down on the ground and began moving his arms and legs around to create the shape of an angel in the snow. Jake tried, and while his version didn't look completely angel like, he laughed at the shape he had made and the twinkle of fun in Oliver's eyes.

Next, they examined the shimmering icicles dangling from the corner of his dad's shed. A single droplet of water clung to the tip of one crystal shard, preparing to fall at any moment.

Beside it, a small, black spider sat proudly in her intricate web, woven with silver thread that glistened in the light. Tiny droplets of water clung to it like scattered diamonds, making it sparkle.

Just then, a red-breasted robin fluttered down into the garden, hopping through the snow in search of food. It paused for a moment, tilting its head to gaze curiously at the strange pair before taking flight once more, and disappearing into the trees above.

"Wow," said Jake. "Everything is so beautiful here. There's so much life and magic. I thought I was the one who lived in a magical world!"

Oliver thought for a moment about all the things in his garden—the things he saw every single day but never really took any notice of. Now, seeing it all through his new friend's eyes made him realise just how truly beautiful it was.

Just then, Jake caught a glimpse of the

coloured lights twinkling through the window from their Christmas tree. His eyes widened with excitement.

"Ohhhhh, can I see it?" he asked eagerly. "I've heard about Christmas trees at school, but I've never, ever, actually seen one!"

"Of course!" Oliver replied with a big smile. "Come closer to the window, and I'll show you everything."

Jake pressed his face close to the glass and Oliver began pointing out all the decorations with enthusiasm.

"I made that one with my mum," he said, gesturing to a large, red ornament covered in glitter and sparkling with tiny diamonds.

"And this one, we bought it at Winter Wonderland last year, that's the coolest place to go if you like huge rollercoasters!"

Oliver pointed to a shiny white snowflake that was spinning and glinting in the light, while Jake wondered what on earth a rollercoaster was!

"And this," he continued, "this was a gift from my Auntie." Hanging gently from a red and green ribbon was a small, delicate silver angel. It twinkled in the lights as if watching over the entire tree.

Each ornament had its own story, and Oliver explained each and every one to Jake, who stood and listened in quiet wonder.

"So, what else makes Christmas special for you?" Jake asked once Oliver had excitedly pointed out every single ornament. "You clearly love it!"

"For me?" Oliver asked, his eyes lighting up. "Well, I suppose it's everything, really! I just love it all! Visiting family and friends, eating all the delicious food we never normally have in the house, the Christmas lights and music everywhere you go, and the happy, warm feeling it gives you in your tummy."

"Is it not about getting presents then?" Jake asked with surprise, "I heard that children loved getting presents?"

Oliver was shocked that the whole time he'd been talking about Christmas he'd actually completely forgotten about the `getting presents´ part.

Well, of course!" Oliver replied. "I LOVE getting presents; who doesn't? But I suppose, now that I think about it, maybe that's actually the least important part. It's the whole magic of Christmas that I love."

Jake tilted his head. "Christmas magic, do you mean?"

"Yes. I suppose so," Oliver said thoughtfully. "It's this feeling you get from being with the people you care about, the excitement of choosing gifts for others, and just believing that something special is in the air. That's what makes Christmas... well, you know, magical."

Jake grew quiet, reflecting on everything Oliver had said. As they stood there, with the glow of the Christmas tree shimmering through the window, Jake felt a sudden warming feeling in his heart—a most peculiar feeling for a snowman.

He glanced down at himself: his snowy body, his twig arms, the green scarf Oliver had carefully wrapped around his neck, and his shiny red heart. Then, slowly, he began to understand.

"That's it," Jake whispered, his voice soft with awe.

"What's it?" Oliver asked, looking at him curiously.

"The reason I came to life," Jake said, more to himself than to Oliver, "it's not just the snow or the way you built me; it's YOU. You're full of Christmas magic, and it's so strong that it brought me to life."

Oliver stared at Jake, his mouth slightly open in surprise. "You really think so?"

Jake nodded, a smile spreading across his face.

"Yes, I do. Christmas is not just about getting presents; it's about the magical feeling it gives you. The love, the joy, the kindness, and you, Oliver, you've got all of that inside you."

Oliver blushed slightly, not quite knowing what to say, but his heart swelled with pride.

Jake looked up at the sky, where the first night stars were beginning to twinkle in the evening air. "I guess that's why I'm here," he said gently. "But I can't stay forever."

Oliver's smile faded. "Do you really have to go?"

Jake nodded. "I do, but thank you for the most wonderful day, I will remember it forever. You've taught me so much about your amazing world."

Oliver couldn't help but feel a little sad. "Will I ever see you again?" He asked quietly.

Jake smiled warmly, his smooth, stone eyes twinkling, the way only magical snowman's can. "Whenever you believe in the magic of Christmas, I'll be right here."

With that, Jake took a step back. His snowy form shimmered briefly, the magic that had brought him to life slowly fading as he settled back into his original shape, a simple snowman, with a green scarf and a red hat standing quietly in the frosty garden.

For a moment, Oliver just stood there, gazing at Jake, but something inside him felt different now.

He didn't feel sad—his heart brimmed with joy. He understood: Christmas wasn't just about decorations, presents, or even snowmen that came to life. It was about the magic inside you, the kind that could last all year long, as long as you believed.

Suddenly, Oliver's tummy rumbled loudly, and he realised just how long he'd been outside. Laughing to himself, he gave one last glance back at Jake, knowing deep down that the magic of Christmas was something he would always carry with him.

With a smile, Oliver turned toward the house, where the glow of the Christmas tree and the delicious smell of dinner welcomed him home.

From that day forward, Oliver knew that as long as he believed, the magic of Christmas would live on, not just in his memories, but in his heart forever.

The End.

The Christmas Adventure

The Christmas Adventure

"So, Mum, can we, can we?" Dylan jumped up and down excitedly. Today was the 1st of December and he had been waiting patiently for what felt like forever, to finally put up their Christmas decorations.

Dylan loved the run-up to Christmas. He loved the colourful lights, the cheerful festive music, and the cold, snowy weather.
He loved cozy evenings in with his family, playing board games or watching TV. And he couldn't wait to help bake tasty treats like sausage rolls and mince pies, then, of course, help to eat them all too!

Everything just felt so magical at this time of year.

"Okay then," his mother laughed, "you've waited long enough. Go upstairs to the loft and find the Christmas bag, then we'll be ready for when your dad gets home."

"Okay!" Dylan replied happily and skipped upstairs.

Dylan loved venturing up into the loft. Even though the air smelt musty, and the floorboards creaked beneath his feet, he always felt like an explorer on a mission to uncover lost treasure.

He scanned the boxes and boxes of forgotten items, stacked high and covered in dust, until he saw the familiar red bag that contained their Christmas decorations.

"Bingo!" he said. Dylan dragged the bag across the floor to the top of the stairs, all ready for his dad to bring down when he arrived home. "I may as well explore some more while I wait," he thought to himself.

Dylan looked around, his eyes landing on a large, dusty trunk in the corner. He hurried over, and with a bit of effort, pushed open the heavy lid, revealing a selection of old clothes, hats, shoes and other intriguing items.

First he found a black pirate hat, faded but still cool, with a feather sticking out of the side. Grinning, he put it on, feeling like a daring explorer setting off on a new adventure.

He dug deeper into the trunk and pulled out a weathered, rolled-up map. Dylan unrolled it carefully and spread it out on the floor. It was crinkled at the edges, and covered in strange, twisty lines and symbols. It looked like a treasure map!

"X marks the spot," he whispered to himself, tracing a path with his finger.

In his mind he was no longer in the loft, he was lost in the jungle, searching for hidden treasure buried beneath the roots of ancient trees.

His hand bumped into something small and cold. He looked down and saw an old brass compass. Dylan picked it up, watching as the needle wiggled and finally pointed North.

Perfect! Now he could easily navigate through the "wilderness" of the loft. He imagined himself trekking through unknown forests, dodging dangers, and following the path to the hidden treasure marked on his map.

As Dylan roamed further, he found an old, leather-bound book. The cover was worn, and the pages were yellow, but as he flipped through it, he saw page after page of magical creatures. There were dragons, unicorns, and enchanted forests. Dylan felt like a wizard learning secrets that had been lost for centuries.

With each new discovery, Dylan's imagination soared. Every corner of the loft was filled with magic and possibilities.

And then, behind a dusty old box, he spotted something small, shiny, and silver. It was a bell covered with a thin layer of dust. As he held it in his hand, something about it felt strange, different somehow.

Dylan couldn't explain it, but this little bell

seemed more magical than anything else he had found so far. Without thinking, he gave it a shake.

Suddenly, the air shimmered around him. The loft began to spin, the dusty boxes blurring together. Before he could blink, Dylan found himself standing in a completely different world. He gasped.

Before him was the most magical village he had ever seen. It was Santa's Village, and it looked like something out of a dream.

The ground was covered in a thick blanket of sparkling, white, snow. Twinkling lights hung from every rooftop, casting a warm glow on the cobblestone streets, and the air smelled of cinnamon and freshly baked cookies.

Elves dressed in bright red and green suits darted around, carrying presents and decorations, laughing as they worked. In the distance, Dylan could hear the faint jingling of sleigh bells.

Towering above the village was a grand workshop, with colourful smoke curling from its chimney.

The sound of hammers and saws echoed from within as the elves busily prepared the toys for Christmas.

Suddenly, a small group of elves appeared in front of him, their faces beaming with excitement. "You must be Dylan!" one of them said with a giggle. "We've been expecting you!"

"Expecting me?" Dylan asked, confused. The elves nodded eagerly, took his hand, and led him through the village.

As they walked, he marvelled at the beauty around him. Snowflakes that looked like delicate crystals fell from the sky. Reindeer pranced and played happily in a nearby field. Quaint red and green houses were decorated with wreaths of holly, and every window seemed to glow from within with the warmth of Christmas spirit.

"Come on, we're almost here!" one of the elves said, tugging at his sleeve.

They stopped in front of a cozy-looking house with a bright red door. It was Santa's house. Dylan felt his heart race with excitement as the door opened, and there stood Santa Claus himself! His rosy cheeks and kind eyes twinkled as he smiled down at Dylan.

"Welcome," Santa said in a deep, warm voice. "I see you found my magic bell."

Dylan nodded, still too amazed to speak. Santa gestured for him to come inside, and they all gathered beside the fire. The room was filled with the warming scent of pine trees and hot chocolate. Santa sat down on a large, comfy-looking red couch and motioned for Dylan to sit down next to him.

"You see, Dylan," Santa began, "the bell you found is very special. It's not just any old bell, it's the Christmas bell. It brings those who ring it to the heart of Christmas, but it can't be rung by just anyone."

Dylan looked down at the bell, still clutched in his hand, understanding now why it had felt so magical before.

Santa continued. "Many children believe Christmas is only about presents and material things, but the true magic of Christmas isn't found there. It's found in kindness, in giving, and in the love that we share with our family and friends. Only children who have the true magic of Christmas in their hearts get to come and spend a day at the heart of Christmas."

As Santa spoke, Dylan felt a warmth growing in his chest. He thought about his family and how they always spent lots of time together, especially during the holidays, laughing and sharing stories. To him, that was what made Christmas special.

Santa smiled kindly. "You've been a good boy all year, Dylan, and you have the true spirit of Christmas in your heart. So, as a reward, you get to spend the whole day here, in Santa's Village."

Santa stood up, his red coat swishing as he gestured towards the door.

"Let my elves show you around."

Dylan's heart soared as the elves led him outside into the snow-covered village. The first stop was Santa's workshop. Long tables stretched out as far as the eye could see, filled with toys in every stage of creation: Dolls, trains, cars, and action figures, all handmade with love and care.

The elves eagerly showed him how they carved the wooden toys, stitched teddy bears, and painted the tiny little details on the cars and trains.

"Would you like to help?" one of the elves asked, handing Dylan a paintbrush and a small silver car.

Dylan nodded eagerly and carefully painted red flames down the side.

After the workshop, the elves took him to the reindeer stables. His eyes widened in awe when he saw Rudolph, Dasher and Dancer all casually taking a drink of water from a big, shiny silver bowl with red trim.

"Do you want to play fetch with them?" an elf asked, tossing Dylan a red rubber ball. "The reindeer love playing fetch."

Dylan laughed as he threw the ball and watched the reindeer chase after it in the snow, then come back to nuzzle him affectionately afterwards. He couldn't believe he was playing fetch with Santa's very own reindeer!

As the day went on, Dylan's excitement grew and grew. The elves showed him all around the village, each part seeming more magical than the last.

Finally, the elves led him into a cozy little cottage, the smell of chocolate and freshly baked cookies filled the air. Inside was Mrs Claus, standing by the oven with a warm smile on her face.

"Ah, you must be Dylan," she said, pulling

out a tray of the most delicious-looking cookies he had ever seen. "Would you like to try one?"

Dylan nodded excitedly, and when he bit into the cookie, it was like tasting pure happiness. It was sweet, warm, and filled with love. Mrs Claus winked at him. "A little bit of love goes into each one. That's the secret ingredient, you know."

After a truly magical day, Dylan felt a tug on his heart as he realised his adventure would soon be coming to an end.

Santa appeared once more, his face glowing with kindness. "Take care, Dylan," Santa said, placing a large, caring, hand on his shoulder. "The world is a better place with little boys like you in it. Make sure you always remember the magic you've seen here today, and the true spirit of Christmas will always be with you."

With a final smile from Santa, everything around Dylan began to swirl in a flurry of sparkling snow.

When the snow cleared, he found himself back in his dusty loft. His dad's voice echoing up from the stairs. "Dylan! Have you found the decorations yet?"

Dylan looked around and saw the big red bag waiting beside the top of the stairs. "Yes, Dad, they're here," he stammered.

Dylan was still in shock and couldn't quite believe what had just happened. Had he really just been transported to Santa's village, or had he imagined it all?

He tried to shrug off his confusion, gave his dad a big, warm hug, and they both made their way downstairs to begin decorating the Christmas tree together.

Dylan began pulling out the ornaments and passing them to his mum, dad, and brothers. Each decoration reminding one of them of a special Christmas story that they then just had to share. As they hung bauble after bauble, the room filled with chatter and laughter, and soon his earlier adventure began to feel like a distant dream.

Maybe it had just been his imagination running wild. Maybe he hadn't really visited Santa's Village. But then again, everything had felt so real, so magical; he couldn't believe he could have made it all up in his head.

Finally, when they thought the bag was empty, Dylan reached in one last time. His hand brushed against something cold and smooth at the very bottom. His heart skipped a beat as he pulled out a small, silver bell. It gleamed in the light, exactly like the one he'd found in the loft earlier that day—the same bell that had taken him on the magical journey to Santa's Village.

Dylan's breath caught in his throat as he stared at the bell, the warmth of Santa's words filling him again. He wasn't imagining it. It had happened. He had been to the heart of Christmas, and this bell was the proof.

"Look what I've found!" Dylan said excitedly, showing the bell to his family.

They all admired it, thinking it was a pretty decoration, but Dylan knew it meant so much more.

He carefully hung the bell on the tree, placing it right at the front where the lights would make it twinkle. As it swayed gently on the branch, Dylan felt a happy glow inside him, spreading from his chest to his fingertips.

It wasn't just from the bell; it was from the love and joy all around him, the laughter of his family, and the happiness they shared as they decorated the tree together.

And as he sat back and admired their tree, the silver bell twinkling at him, Dylan knew, deep down, that he had been a part of something truly special. The magic was real. And with it came the greatest gift of all, the joy of spending Christmas with the people he loved.

The End.

This Christmas, remember that the greatest gifts aren't wrapped in paper but in kindness, love, and the joy you bring to others. Keep believing in the magic—it's all around you!

Merry Christmas

Printed in Great Britain
by Amazon